The Creation Seri
A Bible-based Rea

CW00348482

A Beautiful Garden

Carole Leah
and Sharon Rentta

NOTE TO PARENTS AND TEACHERS

The Creation Series consists of eight books based on the Genesis account in the Bible. This is the eighth book and has been written from a Christian viewpoint. It is intended to be read *to* 3-4 year olds. The series prepares children to read and extend their vocabulary. In this book children can develop and practise preparatory skills for reading as well as realise God's immense love.

BIBLE REFERENCES

All Bible references are in bold throughout and are as follows: p8: Genesis 2:16; p14: Genesis 3:7-8; p16: Genesis 3:11.

ENCOURAGE CHILDREN TO:

*   Talk about the illustrations and retell the story in their own words.
*   Count and name the different kinds of fruits around them.
*   Draw a picture of their own garden or one they have seen.
*   Memorise the Bible verse and its reference (see page 24).
*   Feel the textures of different clothes, e.g. smooth, hard, soft, rough.
*   Talk about how they can please God, e.g. by doing what is right and by obeying their dad and mum.
*   Ensure that the children know the meaning of all these words: *disobeyed* (did not do what was told); *fig* (a dark fruit that grows in warm countries); *flaming* (brightly burning); *forgive* (to be kind to someone when they have done us wrong); *knowledge* (things we know); *sin* (doing wrong); *skins* (the furry coverings of animals); *slither* (to creep, crawl or slide); *spoiled* (messed up).

Carole Leah became a Christian at a youth camp when she was seventeen years old while reading a Gideon New Testament. She felt called to write these books so that young children would learn the truth about God while also developing their reading and vocabulary skills. Several people have worked alongside Carole as she wrote this material but she would like to especially dedicate these books to the memory of her dear friend Ruth Martin who gave so much support.

All scripture quotations in this publication are from the Good News Translation in Today's English Version - Second Edition Copyright © 1992 by American Bible Society. Used by Permission.
Text copyright © Carole Leah. Illustrations copyright © Sharon Rentta.
ISBN: 978-1-84550-536-3 Published by Christian Focus Publications, Geanies House, Fearn, Tain, Ross-shire, IV20 1TW, Scotland, U.K.
www.christianfocus.com
Picture on page 24: Taken by Adrian Pingstone in June 2005 and released to the public domain.

Daniel, Joy and Todd are at playschool.

The children are planting a tree.
They are using little trowels to dig a big hole.

Look for the butterflies!

Can you find pictures of more than 10 butterflies
in this book?

Did you know that butterflies make glue to stick
their eggs onto leaves of plants?

A long time ago, God planted

a beautiful garden in Eden.

Adam and Eve, the first people,

lived in the garden.

They kept the garden beautiful for God.

God wanted Adam and

Eve to live on the Earth for ever.

He had special plans for them.

A river flowed through the garden.

All kinds of beautiful fruit trees grew everywhere.

In the middle of the garden were

two very special trees.

One was the tree of life.

The other was the tree of

the knowledge of good and evil.

God often walked in the garden.

He loved to talk with Adam and Eve.

'...You may eat the fruit of any tree

in the garden,' said God.

'But don't eat fruit from the tree of

the knowledge of good and evil.

If you do eat that fruit, you will die.'

A snake was in the garden.

The snake told lies to Eve about

the tree of knowledge of good and evil.

'Eat the fruit from this tree and

you will not die,' the snake said.

'You will be like God and

know what is good and what is evil.'

The tree was very beautiful and

the fruit looked very good to eat.

Eve thought it would be wonderful

to be like God.

Eve ate some of the fruit and

gave some to Adam.

He ate it.

Adam and Eve disobeyed God.

This was how sin came into the world.

Sin changed everything.

Adam and Eve wanted to cover themselves.

They **sewed fig leaves together and covered themselves.**

That evening they heard the Lord God walking in the garden...

Adam and Eve were afraid **...and they hid from God among the trees.**

God called out to Adam.

God knew what had happened.

God wanted Adam and Eve to come and

own up.

'...**Did you eat the fruit...** from the tree of

the knowledge of good and evil?' asked God.

Adam said, 'It was Eve, she gave it to me.'

Eve said, 'It was the snake, it tricked me.'

They had all done something wrong, so

bad things began to happen.

God made the snake slither on the ground.

God spoke to Adam and Eve.

'Having babies will be hard for you, Eve.'

'Growing food will be hard for you, Adam.'

Thorny plants and weeds began to grow.

Animals, people and plants began to die.

God made clothes out of animal skins for

Adam and Eve.

He sent them out of the garden.

Adam and Eve were very sad.

God still loved them but

they were not close to him anymore.

Angels with a flaming sword kept Adam and

Eve away from the tree of life.

God's plans for Adam and Eve were spoiled.

They could not live on the Earth for ever.

This is what sin did.

It spoiled everything that

God had made but...

... Father God sent his only Son, Jesus Christ,

from heaven to put things right.

He came to die to take away our sin.

He came alive to bring us close to God.

If we come to Jesus and

own up, God will forgive us.

He will take away our sinful

thoughts, words and actions.

Now, we can live with God for ever and ever.

Now, Todd, Daniel and Joy are very happy.

...God loved the world so much that

he gave his only Son...

John, chapter 3, verse 16